SCOTTISH
PROVERBS

SCOTTISH PROVERBS

Compiled by
The Editors at
Hippocrene Books

Illustrated by
Shona Grant

Foreword by
Helen MacRobert Galazka, D. Min.

HIPPOCRENE BOOKS, INC.
New York

For information, address:
HIPPOCRENE BOOKS, INC.
171 Madison Avenue
New York, NY 10016

ISBN 0-7818-0648-8

Printed in the United States of America

EDITOR'S NOTE

These proverbs have been collected and carefully edited to reflect the language spoken in Scotland at the turn of the century. The tone, lifestyle and spirit of the Scottish nation years ago resonates in the colloquial nature of the proverbs.

Because the spelling is quite different from contemporary English language, many of the words are not immediately recognizable. A glossary is provided for this reason and should bring some relief to the occasionally stumped reader. Additionally, there are various contextual notes provided to aid the reader's understanding of a proverb's true nature.

FOREWORD

Proverbs are part of the folklore on which a country builds its identity. They can reveal a great deal of the national character. Scottish proverbs vary from district to district, reflecting the pursuits of the particular population.

In the Southwest and in Ayrshire particularly, people are close to the land and their sayings take on a rural character. They are down to earth and sometimes crude:

"She was a guid goose, but an ill gaislin."
"A cock is crouse on his ain midden."

In the Northeast and on the Islands, the Scottish fishermen, those who "go down to the sea in ships and do business in great waters," set the tone. Facing danger everyday, they tend to be intensely religious and feel close to God. Life for them is a struggle with the elements and their language and philosophy reflect this. Their life may be changing, but their traditions remain, as do their values. They are not afraid to talk of death:

"There's no medicine for fear."
"He'll no' scratch an auld pow,"
(He won't scratch an old head).

In towns and large cities such as Glasgow, an emphasis is on money and the making of it:

"Pay as ye gang, and if ye canna pay, dinna gang."
"Mony hands, mak licht wark."

And with this, an outspoken attitude towards one another's foibles:

"His room is better than his company"
"The Smoke o' ma ain hoose is better than the fire o' yours."

The 'deoch an doris' (similar to a whiskey and soda) is part of the worker's social life with warnings against excess:

"A red nose maks a ragged back."
"Drink little that ye may drink long."

Edinburgh is more concerned with sophistication in its proverbs, and its influences reach southward to the quiet Border country.

"Meat feeds and cloth cleeds, but manners mak' a man."

"A' that's said in the ha' shouldna be telt in the kitchen."

"He that teaches himsel' has a fuil for his master."

The Highlands, home of the mystic, produce proverbs with religious and moral content.

"I theekit ma hoose in the calm weather."

"Envy is the rack of the soul and the torture of the body."

What distinguishes many Scottish proverbs is their humor. For people in a poor country, fighting unpredictable weather and possessing few natural resources, humor can be a secret weapon. Surprisingly, the Scot tends to joke about what threatens him, such as death:

"Be happy while you're living for you're a long time dead."

Or poverty:

"A sillerless man gangs quick through the market."

This kind of satirical humor is bestowed upon women as well. Historically, the Scots shared the ancient fear that women were different and carried 'mana,' the mysterious power that could bring bad luck to certain enterprises like fishing. Many proverbs reflect this philosophy of a bygone age when women were homebound and with few rights:

"A tocherless dame sits lang at hame."

"Flees and a girnin wife are wakefu' bedfellows."

The grudging acquiescence that woman may be a creature to be reckoned with is met with male chauvinism.

"A rich man's wooing need seldom be a long one."

"She waited for the runners but the walkers went by."

"He who's rich when he's married may be poor when he's buried."

The Scot is at heart a philosopher, particularly when he is drinking. It is then, too, that the sentimentality of which is he ashamed finds expression. He will sing of his love and of his native land which frequently he has to leave far behind.

H.V. Morton tells of an incident outside a pub in Dumfres after a Burns night, celebrating the poet's January 25th birthday. The poet's health and immortal memory had been toasted many times and one of the guests, very inebriated, had become tearfully sentimental, remembering that they were at the very spot where "puir auld Robbie lay down and deed." He quoted the poet in word and in song, and remarked, "Ye maybe think I'm a poet. Not me, I'm just an ordinary chap, but Burns is different. What he says is a sae true." Scots love real people and despise the braggart.

You hear this in 'the rank is but the guinea stamp; the man's the gowd.' There is no false immodesty: "The common man, though e'er sae puir is king o' men." And this he believes is the gift of his Scottishness. He is a special breed, set apart from his neighbors over the Border:

> "A Scots mist will wilt an Englishmen to the skin."
>
> "Ye manna tramp on the Scots thistle."

He asserts, there's no mony better than us, an they're a' deid. In his uninhibited moments, he has a pride that evokes the toast, "Here's tae us, wha's like us? Deil the ane."

Helen G. MacRobert Galazka, D. Min.

Proverbs

He that laughs at his ain joke
spoils the sport o' it.

Bear wealth, poverty will bear itself.

Nane can play the fuil as weel as
a wise man.

Even the langest day
will hae an end.

He's a hame devil and a causey saint.
(awful at home, charming outside)

Oot o'debt, oot o' danger.

Sudden freendship,
sure repentance.

When drink's in, wit's oot.

Live weel,
an' dreid nae shame.

Licht burdens
brak nae banes.

A drink is shorter than a tale.

Drink little,
that ye may drink long.

His heid is fu' o' bees.
(said of a drunk)

God sends meat
an' the de'il sends cooks.

A Scots mist will weet an Englishman
tae the skin.

Law's costly, tak a pint an' 'gree.

Ill-will ne'er spak weel.

Be happy while you're livin,
for you're a lang time deid.

A man that is warned
is hauf armed.

Every man's tale is guid
till anither's be tauld.

There is mony a true tale tauld in jest.

Confession
is gude for the saul.

*Better be deid
than oot o' fashion.*

Necessity has no law.

A guid goose indeed
but she was an ill gaislin.
(she improved with age)

He has licked the butter off my bread.

His room is better than
his company.

He has gotten a bite on his
ain bridle.

Dirt parts good company.

*Law-makers shou'd na be
law-breakers.*

Must is a king's word.

He that teaches himsel
has a fuil for his maister.

A rich man's wooing need
seldom be a long one.

He can lie
as weel as a dog can lick a dish.

He brings a staff to brak his ain hert.
(he sets himself up for a broken heart)

It's the best spoke i' your wheel.

It is hard to sit in Rome
an' fight wi' the pope.

Lie for him and he'll swear for you.

He has ae face to God
an' anither to the de'il.

I theekit ma hoose in the guide weather.
(prepared early for death)

The more noble the more humble.

There is little ill said
that is not ill ta'en.

The book o' maybes
    is very braid.

Ne'er let on,
but laugh i' your ain sleeve.

A' that's said i' the ha'
should na be telt i' the kitchen.

Ye're a gude seeker but an ill finder.

They that drink langest live langest.

What may be done at any time
will be done at no time.

He that cheats me aince, shame fa' him;
if he cheats me twice, shame fa' me.

When freends meet,
herts warm.

A burnt bairn dreids the fire.
(experience is a good teacher)

He that gets, forgets,
but he that wants, thinks on.

Confessed faults are half mended.

Envy is the rack of the soul and
the torture of the body.

Laws catch flies, but let hornets go free.

When the hert is full
the tongue will speak.

Weapons bode peace.

Wit in a poor man's heid an' moss on a
mountain avails naethin'.

The best surgeon
is he of the soul.

Man's best candle
is his understanding.

Ye should be king o' your word.

The devil's a busy bishop in
his own diocese.

He that deals in dirt
has aye foul fingers.

A dry lent, a fertile year.

An ill plea should
be weel pled.

A nod from an honest man
is enough.

Cutting out well
is better than sewing up well.

Lifeless, faultless.

A day to come seems longer than
a year that's gone.

Better sma' fish than nae fish.

He'll no' scratch an auld pow.
(he'll die young)

Listen to me
but look to yourself.

A fu' purse never lacks freends.

Ne'er rode ne'er fell.

I'll go doon through him like
a dose o' salts.
(she'll make her point)

Better spared than ill spent.

Learn young,
learn fair;
learn auld,
learn mair.

Ne'er show your teeth
unless you can bite.

Put your hand nae farther than your
sleeve will reach.

There is nae end to an auld sang.

There's nae man sae deif as he that
winna hear.

Honesty has no pride.

He's auld an' cauld
an' ill to lie beside.

*Ae bird i' the haun
is worth ten fleein'.*

Lang may yer lum reek.
(New Year's Eve wish:
to good times ahead)

He'll soon be a beggar that canna say nae.

The more mischief the better sport.

Better to say here it is, than here it was.

We can forgive for debt, but not for unkindness.

What soberness conceals, drunkness reveals.

A dog winna yowl if ye fell him wi'a bane.
(a dog won't cry if you knock him out
with a bone)

The smoke of my own house is better
than the fire of yours.

He that speaks the thing he should not;
shall surely hear the thing he would not.

He canna see an inch afore his nose.

He is poor that canna promise.

It is weel said but wha will bell the cat?
(well said, but who will do the job)

Truth is
the doctor of time.

Cripples are good doers,
break your leg and try.

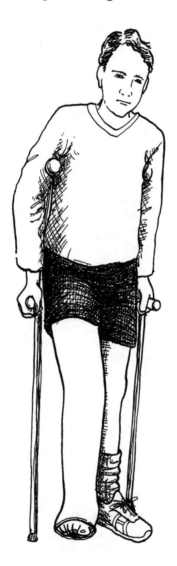

The medicine that hurts the most
is generally the best healer.

Ye're as daft as ye're days auld.
(you are a crazy person)

Penny wise and pound foolish.

Ye wa'd do little for God
if the de'il were deid.

Eat weel is drink weel's brother.

Fair hair may have
foul roots.

*A nod's as good as a wink
to a blind horse.*

A young saint
may prove an old devil.

Auld sin, new shame.

An ill cook shou'd hae
a gude cleaver.

Death defies the doctor.

Every man wishes the water
to his ain mill.

Mony a mickle
maks a muckle.

Ye'll ne'er know a man till
ye do business wi' him.

Do weel and hae weel.

What canna be cured
must be endured.

He that loves law
will soon get his fill of it.

The warld is bound to nae man.

There ne'er was a fair word in flytin'.
(no good word in scolding)

Double drinks
are gude for drouth.

Egotism is
an alphabet of one letter.

Enough's as good as
a feast for a starvin' man.

Mony haws mony snaws.

Better to keep the devil at the door than turn him out of the house.

Ne'er put a sword in a wood man's hand.

Rich fowk hae routh o'freends.

*He that peeks
through a keyhole
may see what
will vex him.*

Naething is difficult
to a weel-willed man.

That's for that,
as butter's for fish.

A new toot o an auld horn.

A nod frae an honest man
is enough.

Forbid a fool a thing an' that he'll do.

Tak time when time is,
for time will awa'.

The lazy man's the beggar's brither.

One may ride a free horse to death.

Better buy than borrow.

She waited for the runners an' the
walkers went by.
(said of a spinster who missed her chance)

A child may have too much of his
mother's blessing.

He that lives upon hope
has a slim diet.

Ye drive the plough afore the oxen.

A man at five
may be a fool at fifteen.

You look liker a thief than a bishop.

A misty morning
may be a clear day.

Ne'er let sorrow
sit near your heart.

Meat feeds and cloth cleeds,
but manners mak a man.

As lang runs the fox as he has feet.

*Tak your thanks to
feed your cat.*

A hungry man sees far.

A tattler is waur than a thief.

It comes to my hand
like the bowl of a pint.
(it comes with ease)

Better to be alone than in ill company.

An illy-willy cow
should have short horns.

There's mony ways to kill a dog
withoot hangin' him.

*Last to bed,
 last out of it.*

A mitten'd cat ne'er was
a good hunter.

Amongst twenty-four fools,
not one wise man.

A man is a lion in his ain cause.

An answer is ae word.

Be a freend to yoursel'
an' ithers will follow.

Better keep weel
than mak weel.

A licht purse maks a heavy hert.

Come wi' the wind
an' gang wi' the watter.

Experience may teach fools.

Envy is cured by true friendship, as
coquetry is by true love.

The grace o' God is gear enough.

Cast na oot the auld watter till the new comes in.

Death is deaf,
and will hear no denial.

As the auld cock craws
the young cock learns.

The devil's cow calves twice a year.

Ne'er let the nose blush for the sins o' the mooth.

That may be and swine may flee, but they're not everyday birdies.

Correct coontin' keeps freends lang
the gither.

A gude fellow has a costly name.

A handfu' o' trade
is worth a gowpen o'gowd.

At open doors, dogs come in.

The rank is but the guinea stamp;
the man's the gawd.
(status doesn't matter in the character of
a man)

A bawbee cat may look at a king.

All things thrive but thrice.

When the well's fu' it will rin ower.

Wood in the wilderness an'
strength in a fool.

Auld sparrows are
ill to tame.

He wha's poor when he's married,
shall be rich when he's buried.

A wee hoose
has a wide mooth.

They are a' gude that are far awa'.

They that lay down for love should rise
for hunger.

It is a silly flock whar the ewe
bears the bell.

Half a tale is enough for a wise man.

The cure may be
worse than the disease.

She hasn't room inside her
for a rheumatic pain.
(said of a thin woman)

There is a time to look agley,
an a time to look even.

When poverty comes in at the door
freendship flees oot at the window.

Swear by your burnt shins.

Take a man by his word and
a cow by his horns.

There is a measure in all things.

A woman is best when
she is openly bad.

*Ye needn't poor watter
    on a drooned mouse.*

That's but ae doctor's opinion.

Twa dochters an' a back-door are three
stark thieves.

Grin when ye win, and laugh when
ye lose.

There's nae medicine for fear.

It is weel that oor fauts are na written on
oor faces.

Keep your tongue within
your teeth.

Tramp on a snail and she'll shoot out her horns.

Put your finger in the fire an' say it was
your fortune.

The more noble
the more humble.

There's none without a fault.

A gude watch prevents harm.

Painters an' poets
hae liberty to lie.

Drunk at night and
dry next morning.

Ill herds make fat wolves.

Pride and grace ne'er dwell
in one place.

Spilt ale is waur than watter.

The day has sight,
the night has ears.

Sma' winnings can mak
a heavy purse.

She looks as if butter wadna melt in
her mou'.

A red nose makes a ragged back.

If you don't see the bottom,
don't wade.

The mou' that lies slays the saul.

The greatest clerks are not the
wisest men.

We are bound to be honest
but not to be rich.

Ye have come a day efter the fair.

When wine sinks,
words soom.

When your neighbor's hoose is in danger
tak care o' your ain.

*Fleas an' a girnin' wife are
wakefire bedfellows.*

Wonder lasts but nine nichts in a
sma' toon.

A guid tale is na the waur to be
twice tauld.

Now's now and the Yule's in winter.

The wise mak jests an' fools
repeat them.

If and *and*
spoil mony a guid charter.

You should be king of your word.

A sillerless man gangs fast
through the market.
(a man without money doesn't take long
at the market)

A tocherless dame sits lang at home.

A cock is crouse on his ain midden.

A wee moose can creep under a great corn stack.

The mare the merrier,
the fewer the better cheer.

A new besom sweeps clean.

He was the bee that made the honey.
(he is the provider)

Bitin' an' scartin'
is Scots fowk's wooin.

Weelcome is the
best dish i' the kitchen.

Daffin' does naethin'.

He has feather'd his nest, he may flee
when he likes.

He that wad eat the kernel maun crack
the nut.

Want o' wit is warse than want o' wealth.

Ye maunna tramp on the Scots thistle.
(don't put a Scotsman down)

Keep your breath to cool your crowdie.
(don't talk unneccessarily)

Many hands make licht wark.

Sorrow an' ill weather come
unsent for.

We'll ne'er ken the worth o' the watter
till the well gaes dry.

Ye hae the wrang soo by the lug.

Guid fowk are scarce,
tak care of yersel'.

A wee bush is better than nae bield.

Guid gear gangs in wee buik.
(good things come in small packages)

Pay as you go,
if you canna pay dinna go.

Ae hour's cauld will suck oot seven
years' heat.

There's nane better than us,
they're a' deid.

That's my tale, what's yours.

Envy ne'er does a good turn but when it
meets an ill ae.

GLOSSARY OF TERMS

Agly — Ugly
Aince — Once
'Bell the cat' — Do the job
Besom — Broom
Bield — Shelter
Braid — Broad, big
Brak — Break
Brither — Brother
Buik — Bulk
Coontin' — Counting
Crouse — Arrogant
Daffing — Teasing
Deid — Dead
Deif — Deaf
De' il — The Devil
Dochters — Daughters
Dreid — Dread
Drouth — Drought
Flytin' — Scolding

Fowk — Folk
Gang — Go, goes
Gear — Material
Girning — Complaining
Gowd — Gold
Guid — Good
Ha' — Hall; perhaps a drinking hall
Hert — Heart
Ken — Know
Kirk — Church
Lang — Long
Licht — Light
Liker — More like
Lum — Chimney
Mair — More
Maun — Must
Midden — Compost pile, in farm yard
Mony — Many
Naethin — Nothing
Pow — Head
Reek — Smoke
Routh — Rounds
Sae — So
Saul — Soul
Scarting — Scratching
Sillerless — Shilling -less
Spak — Spoke
Tattler — A tattle-tale

Thistle — A spiny flower prominent in
        Scotland; Scotch Thistle

Tocherless — Dowry-less

Wad — Would

Waur — Worse

Watter — Water

Weel — Well

Weet — Wet

Wrang — Wrong

Love Poetry from the Gaelic Tradition...

SCOTTISH LOVE POEMS
A Personal Anthology
edited by Lady Antonia Fraser, re-issued edition
Lady Antonia Fraser has selected her favorite poets from Robert Burns to Aileen Campbell Nye and placed them together in a tender anthology of romance. Famous for her own literary talents, her critical writer's eye has allowed her to collect the best loves and passions of her fellow Scots and put them into a book that will find a way to touch everyone's heart.
220 pages • 5 ½ x 8 ¼ • 0-7818-0406-X • $14.95pb

IRISH LOVE POEMS
edited by Paula Redes
A beautifully illustrated anthology that offers an intriguing glimpse into the world of Irish passion, often fraught simultaneously with both love and violence. For some contemporary poets this will be their first appearance in a U.S. anthology. Included are poets Thomas Moore, Padraic Pearse, W.B. Yates, John Montague, and Nuala Ni Dhomnaill.

Gabriel Rosenstock, famous poet and translator, forwards the book, wittily introducing the reader to both the collection and the rich Irish Poetic tradition.
176 pages • 6 x 9 • illustrated • 0-7818-0396-9 • $14.95

Language Guides...

DICTIONARY OF SCOTS WORDS AND PHRASES IN CURRENT USE
James A.C. Stevenson
Scots is a living language and this dictionary covers the most widely-used words and expressions. Entries are arranged in fifteen sections, each of which deals with some aspect of everyday life in Scotland (eating and drinking, people, health, law). A key is provided to indicate the various contexts (colloquial, literary, etc.) in which the words are commonly used. Examples of actual usage in contemporary writing, newspapers, periodicals and conversation are included to illustrate the meanings of the words.
256 pages • 5 ½ x 9 • 1,000 entries • 0-7818-0664-X • $11.95pb • (758) • September 98

SCOTTISH [DORIC]-ENGLISH/ENGLISH-SCOTTISH [DORIC] CONCISE DICTIONARY

Douglas Kynoch

This dictionary is a guide to the Scots language as spoken in parts of the northeastern corner of the country and northern England. Beginning with a brief introduction to spelling, pronunciation, and grammar, it presents a two-way lexicon of North-East Scots with 12,000 significant entries.

186 pages • 5 ½ x 8 ½ • 12,000 entries • 0-7818-0655-0 • $12.95pb • (705) • September 98

SCOTTISH GAELIC-ENGLISH/ENGLISH-SCOTTISH GAELIC DICTIONARY

R.W. Renton & J.A. MacDonald

Scottish Gaelic is the language of a traditional people, over 75,000 strong. This dictionary provides the learner or traveler with a basic, modern vocabulary and the means to communicate in a quick fashion.   This dictionary includes 8,500 modern, up-to-date entries, a list of abbreviation and appendix of irregular verbs, a grammar guide, written especially for students and travelers.

416 • pages • 5 ½ x 8 ½ • 0-7818-0316-0 • $8.95pb

BEGINNER'S WELSH

Heini Gruffudd

The Welsh language, with its rich culture and heritage, has successfully survived to this day. More than half a million people speak the language throughout the country in Wales, while thousands in England, the U.S. and elsewhere have continued to keep the language alive. Beginner's Welsh is an easy to follow guide to grammar, pronunciation and rules of the language. A clear and concise introduction to Welsh politics, the economy, literature, and geography preface the language guide.

Heini Gruffudd is an experienced teacher of Welsh. His best selling language books for adults are well-known in Wales. He currently works as a Welsh language and literature lecturer at the University of Wales, Swansea.

ETYMOLOGICAL DICTIONARY OF SCOTTISH-GAELIC

416 pages • 5 ½ x 8 ½ • 6,900 entries • 0-7818-0632-1 • $14.95pb • (710)

IRISH-ENGLISH/ENGLISH-IRISH DICTIONARY AND PHRASEBOOK
160 pages • 3 3/4 x 7 • 1,400 entries/phrases • 0-87052-110-1 • $7.95pb • (385)

BRITISH-AMERICAN/AMERICAN-BRITISH DICTIONARY AND PHRASEBOOK
160 pages • 3 3/4 x 7 • 1,400 entries • 0-7818-0450-7 • $11.95pb • (247)

Travel Guides..

LANGUAGE AND TRAVEL GUIDE TO BRITAIN
266 pages • 5 1/2 x 8 1/2 • 2 maps, photos throughout, index • 0-7818-0290-3 • $14.95pb • (119)

Cookbooks...

ENGLISH ROYAL COOKBOOK: FAVORITE COURT RECIPES

Elizabeth Craig

Dine like a King or Queen with this unique collection of over 350 favorite recipes of the English royals, spanning 500 years of feasts! Start off with delicate Duke of York Consommé as a first course, then savor King George the Fifth's Mutton Cutlets, and for a main course, feast on Quails a la Princess Louise in Regent's Plum Sauce, with Baked Potatoes Au Parmesan and Mary Queen of Scots Salad. For dessert, try a slice of Crown Jewel Cake, and wash it all down with a Princess Mary Cocktail. These are real recipes, the majority of them left in their original wording. Although this book is primarily a cookery book, it can also be read as a revealing footnote to Court history. Charmingly illustrated throughout.

187 pages • 5 1/2 x 8 1/2 • 0-7818-0583-X • $11.95pb • (723) • May 1998

TRADITIONAL FOOD FROM SCOTLAND: THE EDINBURGH BOOK OF PLAIN COOKERY RECIPES

A delightful assortment of Scottish recipes and helpful hints for the home—this classic volume offers a window into another era.

336 pages • 5 1/2 x 8 • 0-7818-0514-7 • $11.95pb • (620)

TRADITIONAL FOOD FROM WALES

A HIPPOCRENE ORIGINAL COOKBOOK

Bobby Freeman

Welsh food and customs through the centuries. This book combines over 260 authentic, proven recipes with cultural and social history

332 pages • 5 1/2 x 8 1/2 • 0-7818-0527-9 • $24.95 • (638)

CELTIC COOKBOOK: Traditional Recipes from the Six Celtic Lands Brittany, Cornwall, Ireland, Isle of Man, Scotland and Wales

Helen Smith-Twiddy

This collection of over 160 recipes from the Celtic world includes traditional, yet still popular dishes like Rabbit Hoggan and Gwydd y Dolig (Stuffed Goose in Red Wine).

200 pages • 5 1/2 x 8 1/2 • 0-7818-0579-1 • 22.50hc (679)

TRADITIONAL RECIPES FROM OLD ENGLAND

Arranged by country, this charming classic features the favorite dishes and mealtime customs from across England, Scotland, Wales and Ireland.

128 pages • 5 x 8 1/2 • 0-7818-0489-2 • $9.95pb • (157)

THE ART OF IRISH COOKING

Monica Sheridan

Nearly 200 recipes for traditional Irish fare.

166 pages • 5 1/2 x 8 1/2 • 0-7818-0454-X • $12.95pb • (335)